DINOSAUR DISCOVERIES

Smithsonian

DINOSAUR DISCOVERIES

Smithsonian

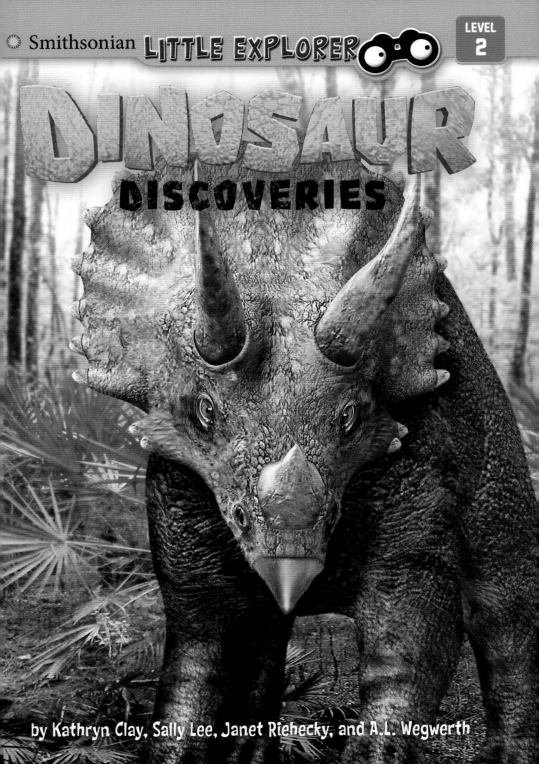

Smithsonian **LITTLE EXPLORER**

LEVEL 2

DINOSAUR
DISCOVERIES

by Kathryn Clay, Sally Lee, Janet Riehecky, and A.L. Wegwerth

CAPSTONE PRESS
a capstone imprint

TABLE OF CONTENTS

APATOSAURUS

DINO FILE

name: Apatosaurus

how to say it: uh-pat-oh-SAW-rus

when it lived: late Jurassic Period, Mesozoic Era

what it ate: plants

size: up to 100 feet (30.5 meters) long
15 feet (4.6 m) tall from the ground to the hips
weighed 33 to 38 tons

Apatosaurus is a
popular dinosaur.
But many people
used to call it another
name—Brontosaurus.

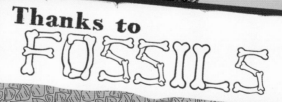

Thanks to
FOSSILS

A fossil is evidence of life from the
past. Fossils of things like bones,
teeth, and tracks found in the earth
have taught us everything we
know about dinosaurs.

PREHISTORIC GIANT

nostrils on
top of head

long neck

small head with
a tiny brain

one large
claw on each
front foot

Apatosaurus was a huge dinosaur. It was as long as two city buses. It weighed as much as five elephants.

Apatosaurus was part of a group of dinosaurs called sauropods. The four-legged dinosaurs had long necks and tails.

strong tail

thick legs

five toes on each foot

A LONG, LARGE TAIL

Apatosaurus's tail was about 50 feet (15 m) long.
That's more than half the length of its body.
The dinosaur's tail was as thick as a trash can
near its body. It ended in a skinny whip.

Allosaurus and
Apatosaurus

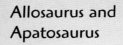

Allosaurus was Apatosaurus's main predator. But Apatosaurus was up to 10 times bigger than Allosaurus.

HEAVY STEPS

Apatosaurus walked on four thick legs.
Its back legs were longer than its front legs.

Apatosaurus had a large claw on each of
its front feet. The dinosaur's feet had five
toes. Thick padding on the bottom of its
feet helped soften its heavy footsteps.

Sauropod trackways in Chile

Over time the mud that dinosaurs walked on turned to stone. Their footprints can still be seen in the stone millions of years later. These fossil footprints are called trackways. They give scientists clues about where dinosaurs lived and how they moved.

Heavy animals like elephants also have padded feet.

LONG NECK

Apatosaurus had a neck that was about 40 feet (12 m) long. A long neck let the dinosaur poke its head into places where its giant body couldn't fit. It could reach food without moving its body. Apatosaurus could stand on dry ground and eat plants growing in muddy swamps.

Apatosaurus couldn't lift its head straight up. It swept its head from side to side.

TINY HEAD

Apatosaurus had a small head. It was about 2 feet (0.6 m) long.

The dinosaur had peglike teeth in the front of its mouth. Apatosaurus used its teeth to strip off leaves and gather plants. There were no teeth in the back of its mouth.

Apatosaurus's nostrils were on top of its head. Scientists once thought this meant it lived in water. Now scientists know more about how Apatosaurus lived. The dinosaur's trackways show that it only lived on land.

Dinosaur trackways made by a relative of Apatosaurus

JURASSIC HOME

Apatosaurus lived in what is now the western United States. It made its home in the states of Colorado, Oklahoma, Utah, Montana, and Wyoming.

This area had warm and dry seasons during the late Jurassic Period. Plants and trees grew easily.

Sauropods first appeared during the Jurassic Period. They were the largest land animals of all time.

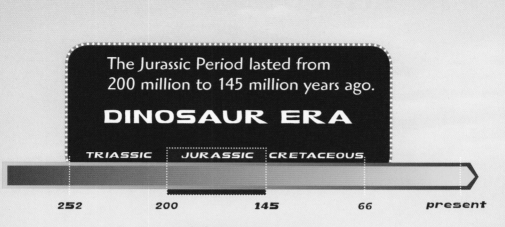

The Jurassic Period lasted from 200 million to 145 million years ago.

DINOSAUR ERA

TRIASSIC　　JURASSIC　CRETACEOUS.

252　　　　200　　　　145　　　　66　　　present

millions of
years ago

BIG EATER

Some scientists think Apatosaurus ate up to 1,000 pounds (454 kilograms) of food each day.

Apatosaurus was an herbivore. This means it ate only plants.

This dinosaur ate conifers, cycads, and ginkgo trees. It also ate low-growing plants such as mosses and ferns.

Gastroliths

Apatosaurus swallowed its food whole. It also swallowed stones called gastroliths. The stones helped grind up the tough plants in the dinosaur's stomach.

LIVING ALONE

Apatosaurus may have lived
alone rather than in herds.
Apatosaurus fossils have never
been found in groups.

Apatosaurus spent most of its day eating.
Because of its huge size, Apatosaurus
had to keep moving to find more food.

The dinosaur's size kept
most predators away.

EGGS AND BABIES

Apatosaurus hatched from an egg smaller than a soccer ball. A female Apatosaurus laid her eggs in a line while walking. Females did not take care of their eggs or babies. Scientists know this because footprints do not show young Apatosauruses traveling with adults.

Most Apatosaurus babies never became adults. They were killed by predators.

Model of a sauropod egg

Apatosaurus babies were less than 2 feet (0.6 m) long. They weighed about 22 pounds (10 kilograms).

MONSTROUS BONES

In 1877 geologist Arthur Lakes was studying
rocks near the Morrison Formation in Colorado.
He found huge bones. Lakes sent some of the
bones to paleontologist Othniel Marsh.

Arthur Lakes

They were "*so monstrous . . . so utterly
beyond anything I had ever read or
conceived possible . . .*"
—from Arthur Lakes's journal

Thousands of fossils from Jurassic dinosaurs have been found in the Morrison Formation. This area of layered rock covers much of the western United States.

Morrison Formation

MIXED-UP NAMES

Marsh believed the bones that Lakes found were from a dinosaur. Marsh named the dinosaur *Apatosaurus* in 1877. Two years later Marsh was studying a larger set of bones. He named this dinosaur *Brontosaurus*.

Elmer Riggs (right) and his assistant studied fossils in his lab.

But Marsh goofed. Paleontologist Elmer Riggs studied Lakes's bones again in 1903. He found the fossils thought to be a young Brontosaurus were really from Apatosaurus. This means the same dinosaur had two different names. The name *Apatosaurus* was used first, so it became the dinosaur's official name.

Elmer Riggs with a Menodus skull

Brontosaurus was popular in books and cartoons such as *The Flintstones*. Most people didn't want the dinosaur's name to be changed. It took nearly 80 years for the name *Apatosaurus* to be accepted by the public.

WRONG HEAD

The first Apatosaurus fossil didn't have a head. A skull found nearby looked too small to belong to such a large dinosaur. Casts of a larger skull were put on Apatosaurus models in museums. But the skull belonged to a different dinosaur—Camarasaurus. For years Apatosaurus models had the wrong heads.

An Apatosaurus skeleton with a Camarasaurus head

Two dinosaur experts thought Apatosaurus had a small head like Diplodocus. They found the right skull in a museum basement. Apatosaurus models have had the right heads since 1934.

Camarasaurus

Camarasaurus was a sauropod that lived during the late Jurassic Period. It was smaller than Apatosaurus. But it had a bigger head.

BRACHIOSAURUS

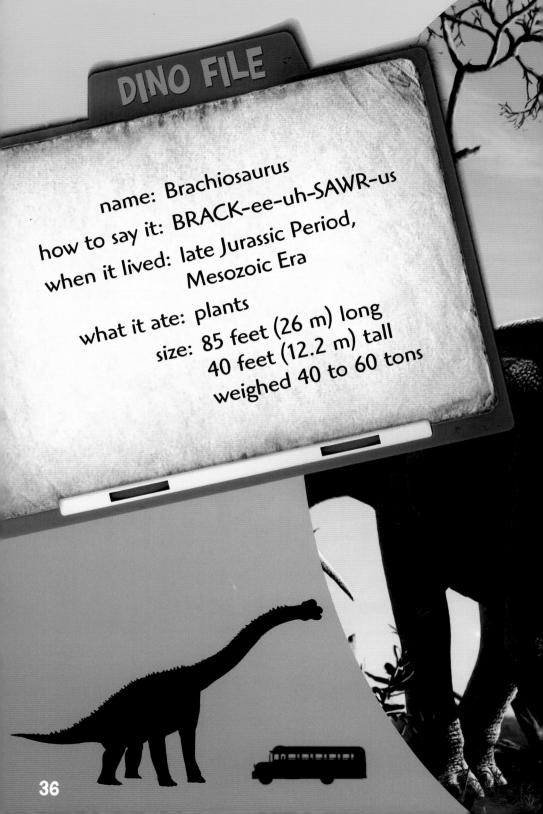

name: Brachiosaurus

how to say it: BRACK-ee-uh-SAWR-us

when it lived: late Jurassic Period,
Mesozoic Era

what it ate: plants

size: 85 feet (26 m) long
40 feet (12.2 m) tall
weighed 40 to 60 tons

Brachiosaurus was one of the largest land animals ever. Unlike the deadly Allosaurus that also lived during this time, Brachiosaurus was a gentle giant.

LONG AND STRONG

Brachiosaurus belonged to a group of
dinosaurs called sauropods. These dinosaurs
had long necks and tails. They walked on
four legs. Other dinosaurs in this group
include Apatosaurus and Diplodocus.

strong tail

shorter
hind legs

BIG BODY, TINY HEAD

Brachiosaurus had a
tiny head compared
to its large body. Inside
its head was an even
smaller brain.

The dinosaur had two nostrils on top of its head. Long ago, scientists thought this meant Brachiosaurus lived in water. This nostril position would have allowed the dinosaur to breathe while its body was underwater. Now scientists know Brachiosaurus lived on land.

Brachiosaurus tracks were found in North America. This shows that the dinosaur lived on land.

LONG NECK

Brachiosaurus's neck was about 18 feet (4.9 m) long. That's as tall as a two-story building! The dinosaur's long neck allowed it to eat leaves from plants and trees.

Though big, the dinosaur's neck was not very heavy. Brachiosaurus's backbones were hollow like a bird's bones are today. Because its bones were so light, Brachiosaurus could move its neck around like a giraffe.

In addition to sauropods like Brachiosaurus, theropods such as Tyrannosaurus rex had hollow bones.

44

STANDING TALL

Brachiosaurus means "arm lizard." The dinosaur was given the name because its front legs were much longer than its hind legs. Other sauropods had long hind legs and shorter front legs.

Brachiosaurus had five toes on each foot. Padding on its feet supported the dinosaur's weight. A sharp claw stuck out from its front feet. Three back toes also had claws.

Scientists think the dinosaur's claws were used to fight off predators or collect food. Brachiosaurus could also use its claws to dig into the ground.

JURASSIC HOME

During the Jurassic Period, the earth was warm and tropical. Plants grew everywhere. Giant dinosaurs such as Camarasaurus and Diplodocus roamed.

Brachiosaurus lived in what is now western North America, in the states of Wyoming, Colorado, and Utah. It made its home in plains and forests.

The Jurassic Period lasted from 200 million to 145 million years ago.

DINOSAUR ERA

TRIASSIC	JURASSIC	CRETACEOUS

252   200   145   66   present

millions of
years ago

DINNER TIME

Brachiosaurus was an herbivore. It ate only plants.

A Brachiosaurus could eat 1,000 pounds (454 kg) of food per day.

Few other animals could reach the dinosaur's food.

Brachiosaurus spent most of its day eating and searching for food. Its long neck allowed it to eat from the tops of trees. Young dinosaurs also ate ferns, conifers, and cycads near the ground.

ROCK STAR

Brachiosaurus had 56 spoonlike teeth. But its teeth weren't used for chewing. Instead, the dinosaur used them to pull leaves off trees.

Brachiosaurus swallowed its food whole. To break up the food, the dinosaur also swallowed rocks called gastroliths. The gastroliths rolled around in the dinosaur's stomach. They helped break down plants into a paste. This made the plants easier to digest.

Several modern birds swallow small bits of gravel and rock to help digest food.

LIVING IN HERDS

Brachiosaurus may have traveled in herds of up to 20 dinosaurs. The herds moved each day to find new food sources.

The dinosaurs tried to walk on dry, flat land. Their heavy bodies could get stuck in muddy ground.

An elephant herd in South Africa

Today many herbivores travel together to find food. Elephants walk up to 16 hours each day to find enough plants to eat.

STAYING SAFE

Because of its large size, Brachiosaurus had few predators. Its long tail could hit hungry meat eaters. Its thick legs could crush enemies that came too close.

Predators tried to eat young dinosaurs. To protect them, the Brachiosaurus herd may have formed a circle. The larger dinosaurs kept the smaller, younger ones safe inside the circle.

Allosaurus

One strike from Brachiosaurus's sharp claws could keep away meat-eating dinosaurs such as Allosaurus.

DINO YOUNG

Like most dinosaurs, Brachiosaurus hatched
from eggs. The dinosaur's eggs were large,
thick, and shaped like soccer balls. When
Brachiosaurus babies were born, they were
only about the size of large cats such as
leopards.

Fossils of young sauropods are rare. In 2007 fossils from a young dinosaur were found in Wyoming. Scientists first thought it was a Diplodocus. Now scientists think it could be a Brachiosaurus.

Some eggs have dinosaur bones inside. The bones help scientists identify what type of dinosaur it was. If there are no bones inside, scientists can sometimes identify the egg by its shape and size.

FINDING FOSSILS

In 1900 paleontologist Elmer Riggs found what was thought to be the first Brachiosaurus fossil in the Morrison Formation in Colorado. But Brachiosaurus was discovered much earlier. Othniel Marsh found the first Brachiosaurus fossil in 1883, but he mislabeled it as a Camarasaurus. Scientists correctly identified the fossil in 1998.

Scientists continue to uncover new information about sauropods and other dinosaurs.

"We now have to . . . re-evaluate what we thought we knew about how dinosaurs worked. . . . We need to start looking for new and different evidence."
—paleontologist Emily Rayfield

A Brachiosaurus skeleton is on display in the National History Museum, Berlin, Germany.

DIE WELT IM OBEREN JURA

LIGHTS, CAMERA, ACTION!

Brachiosaurus has always been a Hollywood favorite. The dinosaur has been featured in many movies, including *Jurassic Park, Jurassic Park III,* and *The Land Before Time.*

In *Jurassic Park,* a Brachiosaurus herd grazes among the trees. But Brachiosaurus stood on its hind legs in the movie. Most scientists agree that the real dinosaur couldn't have done this.

In the movie series *The Land Before Time,* the character Shorty was a Brachiosaurus.

Characters Alan Grant and Ellie Sattler encounter a Brachiosaurus in one of the opening scenes of *Jurassic Park*.

STEGOSAURUS

name: Stegosaurus

how to say it: steg-uh-SAW-rus

when it lived: late Jurassic Period, Mesozoic Era

what it ate: plants

size: 21 to 30 feet (6.4 to 9 m) long

12 feet (3.7 m) tall at the hips

weighed 2 to 3 tons

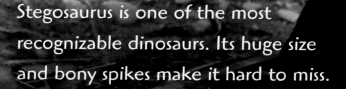

Stegosaurus is one of the most recognizable dinosaurs. Its huge size and bony spikes make it hard to miss.

Stegosaurus lived a very long time ago.
In fact humans live closer in time to
Tyrannosaurus rex than Tyrannosaurus rex
did to Stegosaurus.

THE BONE WARS

The first Stegosaurus fossil was discovered in Colorado in 1876. Othniel Marsh named the dinosaur in 1877. Marsh found Stegosaurus during a time known as the Bone Wars.

Othniel Marsh

Marsh first thought that Stegosaurus might have looked something like a huge turtle.

Colorado

Edward Drinker Cope

Marsh was racing against another dinosaur hunter, Edward Drinker Cope. Each hoped to find the most dinosaurs. Their race led to many discoveries.

The Stegosaurus skeleton Marsh found is at Smithsonian's National Museum of Natural History in Washington, D.C.

SPIKY STEGOSAURUS

bony plates

small skull and brain

narrow,
toothless beak

short front legs

Stegosaurus was one of the first American armored dinosaurs to be discovered.

four-spiked tail

JURASSIC LIFE

Stegosaurus lived during the late Jurassic Period, 150–145 million years ago. Huge dinosaurs like Brachiosaurus and Diplodocus also roamed the land.

Allosaurus was the main predator of the Jurassic Period. Archaeopteryx—an early flying dinosaur—also lived during this time. It shared the sky with flying reptiles, such as pterodactyls, and many insects.

Archaeopteryx

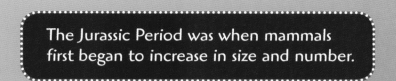

The Jurassic Period was when mammals first began to increase in size and number.

The Jurassic Period lasted from 200 million to 145 million years ago.

DINOSAUR ERA

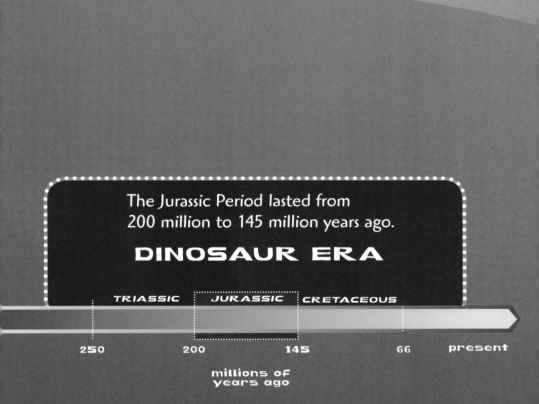

TRIASSIC   JURASSIC   CRETACEOUS

250   200   145   66   present

millions of
years ago

STEGOSAURUS STOMPING GROUND

In the time of dinosaurs, Earth did not look like it does today.

At the beginning of the Triassic Period, there was one supercontinent. It is known as Pangaea. By the Jurassic Period, Pangaea had broken into two continents. One was in the north, and one was in the south.

Earth during the Jurassic Period

Scientists discovered a Stegosaur fossil in Portugal in 2006. It was the first one found outside of North America.

Stegosaurus lived mostly in the northern landmass, which is where part of western North America is today.

The Jurassic Period was very warm and wet. Sea levels were high. Forests full of ferns, cycads, and conifers replaced the deserts of the Triassic Period.

BONY PLATES

Stegosaurus means "roofed lizard." The name comes from early paleontologists who thought the plates looked like shingles on a roof.

Stegosaurus's plates were covered in keratin. That's the same material that human fingernails are made of.

The plates stuck up from the dinosaur's back. They didn't offer any protection to the sides of its body. For this reason scientists believe the plates had purposes besides defense.

SOLAR-POWERED DINOSAUR

Scientists now believe Stegosaurus's plates likely helped the dinosaur keep a regular body temperature.

Some paleontologists think that the plates acted like solar panels for heating.

Without plates, Stegosaurus would have had less area to take in sun or shade.

Blood pumped through the large plates. This gave more area for the blood to flow near the surface of the dinosaur's skin. The body temperature would quickly cool in the shade or warm up in the sun.

With plates, Stegosaurus had more area to take in sun or shade as needed.

SMALL BRAIN

Stegosaurus is known for its small skull and brain. Because of its small brain, some people think Stegosaurus wasn't smart. But the species lived for millions of years. Stegosaurus's brain was the perfect size for its kind to survive a very long time.

Stegosaurus's brain was about the size and shape of a banana. Compared to its huge body, this was tiny!

Meat-eating dinosaurs typically had larger brains than plant-eating dinosaurs like Stegosaurus. Larger brains helped the meat eaters hunt their prey.

PLANT EATER

Stegosaurus was an herbivore.
Herbivores eat plants.

At the tip of its snout was a thin,
toothless beak, much like a turtle's
beak. The beak was used to chop
low-lying bushes and shrubs.

Stegosaurus didn't need a
strong bite for snacking on
plants. An alligator's bite is
13 times stronger than a
Stegosaurus's bite!

The sides of Stegosaurus's mouth had many leaf-shaped teeth. They helped crush plants to be swallowed.

STAYING SAFE

Stegosaurus didn't hunt, but that
doesn't mean it didn't face danger.

If faced with a predator, such as Ceratosaurus, Stegosaurus probably didn't run. It stayed put and tried to protect itself.

Stegosaurus was not known to be a fast or nimble dinosaur. Traveling in herds may have helped keep it safe from predators.

ONE TOUGH TAIL

With its spiky plates, you might think Stegosaurus was well armed against predators. But most paleontologists agree that the back plates didn't provide much protection.

Its powerful spiked tail was probably the dinosaur's best weapon. It looks stiff, but scientists think it was quite flexible.

Stegosaurus could swing its tail fast. It may have used its tail to strike predators.

STEGOSAURUS VERSUS ALLOSAURUS

Paleontologists made an amazing discovery in the spring of 2007. Fossils of an Allosaurus and Stegosaurus were found together in Wyoming. The two dinosaurs appeared to be caught in a fight to the death!

Allosaurus skeleton in the Morrison Formation

Allosaurus claw

Allosaurus was a deadly predator. Another discovery included a Stegosaurus fossil with an Allosaurus bite mark in its neck.

FAMOUS FOSSILS

After millions of years, Stegosaurus became extinct at the end of the Jurassic Period.

Most Stegosaurus fossils have been found in a rocky area of Colorado and Wyoming called the Morrison Formation. It is famous for the number of Jurassic dinosaur fossils discovered there.

This is a fossil from the Morrison Formation in Colorado.

Dinosaur Bone

"The marvel is not that [the dinosaurs] died out, but that they survived so long." —paleontologist Richard Swann Lull

Stegosaurus is Colorado's state fossil because of the many skeleton finds.

TRICERATOPS

name: Triceratops

how to say it: try-SAIR-uh-tops

when it lived: Cretaceous Period, Mesozoic Era

what it ate: plants

size: 25 to 30 feet (7.6 to 9.1 m) long

9 to 10 feet (2.7 to 3 m) tall

weighed 6 to 12 tons

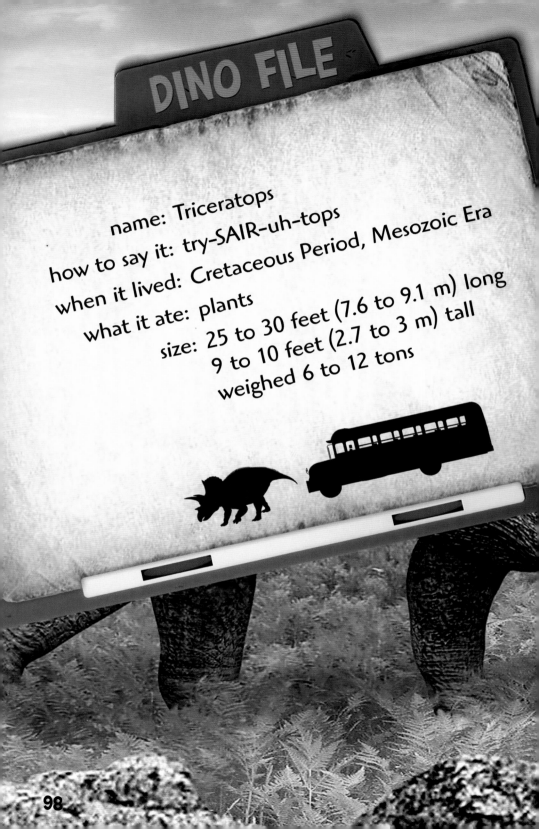

Triceratops roamed North America 68–66 million years ago. Triceratops had a huge head, long horns, and bony frill.

A STRANGE-LOOKING DINOSAUR

Triceratops means "three-horned face." The dinosaur looked a little like today's rhinoceros. Some people even call Triceratops a prehistoric rhinoceros. But the two animals are not related.

short tail

bony frill

long horns
over eyes

small horn
on nose

horned beak

toes covered by
small hooves

GROWING UP

Triceratops hatched from an egg. The baby had large eyes and a short frill.

A young Triceratops's horns curved back. Triangle-shaped spikes grew on the edge of its frill.

Models of an adult and a young Triceratops

Triceratops's skull was up to 8 feet (2.4 m) long.

When Triceratops became an adult, its horns changed direction. They curved forward. The spikes on its frill smoothed together.

A THRILLING FRILL

Triceratops's frill was used
for different things.

✔ The frill likely protected
   Triceratops during an attack.

✔ A male may have used
   his big frill to attract a
   female Triceratops.

✔ The frill may have kept
   Triceratops cool. Heat
   from the dinosaur's body
   could escape off the
   wide frill.

Elephants use their
ears to cool off
in the same way.

MIGHTY HORNS

Below its two long horns, Triceratops had a shorter horn on its nose.

The male Triceratops probably locked horns with other males during battles over a mate.

Female Triceratops likely wanted a mate with long horns. Long horns showed strength and power.

Horns helped Triceratops fight
if attacked. They were sharp enough
to stab predators.

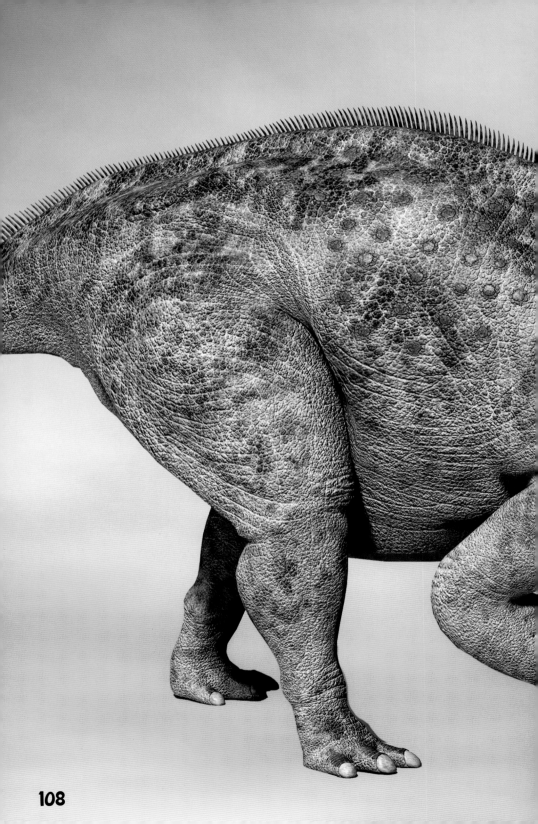

DEFENDING ITSELF

Triceratops was good at protecting itself and its young. A group of Triceratops could have stood shoulder to shoulder. The young were protected behind the wall. No predator could get through the strong wall they made.

If Triceratops charged, even a Tyrannosaurus rex would have been in trouble.

"No species that has ever evolved on land could withstand the full charge of such an animal."
—paleontologist Robert Bakker

STANDING TALL

Scientists used to think Triceratops's legs stuck out on both sides, like a crocodile's legs. Now they think the dinosaur's legs were almost upright. Its legs moved forward and backward in nearly a straight line.

Triceratops could also lock its knees. Its legs wouldn't bend at all.

Many scientists think Triceratops could run 10 to 15 miles (16 to 24 kilometers) an hour.

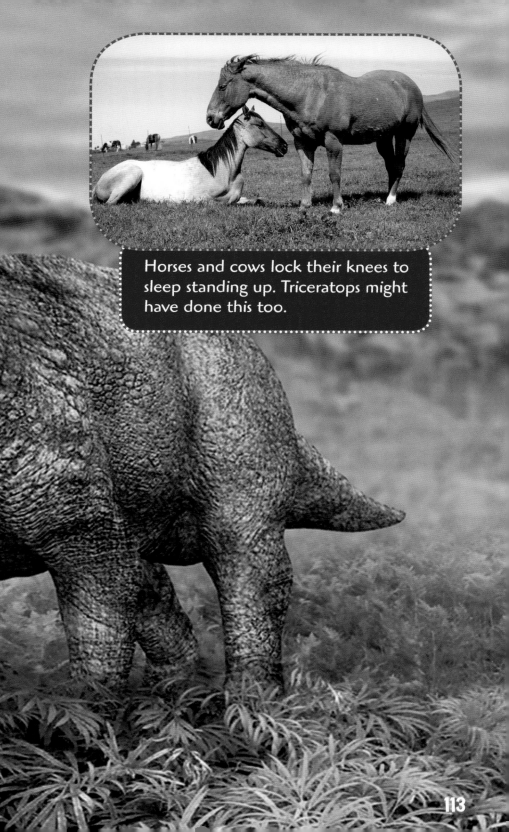

Horses and cows lock their knees to sleep standing up. Triceratops might have done this too.

WHAT'S FOR DINNER?

Triceratops was an herbivore. With its short neck, Triceratops had to eat plants that grew close to the ground.

parrot

The dinosaur had a parrotlike beak for a mouth. It could chomp through hard foods such as conifer needles and branches. Triceratops also grazed on ferns, cycads, and flowering plants.

Triceratops had up to 800 teeth in its mouth. If Triceratops lost a tooth, a new one grew in. It had three to five replacement teeth underneath each tooth.

TRICERATOPS'S WORLD

Triceratops lived during the end of the Cretaceous Period. The world was warmer during this time. Evergreen conifers, ferns, and cycads covered the land. Flowering plants grew for the first time.

Many scientists think Triceratops lived on wide, flat plains. It also looked for food in the forests.

Alamosaurus was a sauropod that lived alongside Triceratops in the southwestern United States.

The Cretaceous Period lasted from 145 million to 66 million years ago.

DINOSAUR ERA

TRIASSIC JURASSIC CRETACEOUS

250   200   145   66   present

millions of
years ago

The average temperature was a few degrees warmer than today.

A shallow sea covered the middle of North America.

117

DISCOVERY

The first Triceratops fossil was a pair of horns. They were found outside Denver, Colorado, in 1887.

Othniel Marsh

Canada

Montana

Wyoming South Dakota

Utah Colorado

Triceratops fossils have been discovered in Alberta and Saskatchewan, Canada. Colorado, Montana, South Dakota, Wyoming, and Utah also have Triceratops fossils.

The horns were sent to Othniel Marsh. He thought they were from a bison. Later more fossils were found. Marsh knew they were from a dinosaur. He named it Triceratops.

More than 100 Triceratops skulls have been found so far.

TRICERATOPS'S RELATIVES

Triceratops was part of a group of dinosaurs called ceratopsians. These dinosaurs had horns and frills.

Pentaceratops

(pen–tuh–SAIR–uh–tops) had a short horn on its nose. The horns over its eyes were long. Its frill had many short spikes.

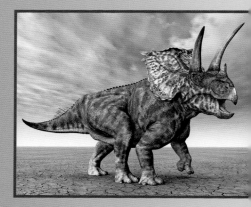

Diabloceratops

(dee–ah–bloh–SAIR–uh–tops) was discovered recently. It had short horns over its eyes and on its nose. Two long spikes grew out of the top of its frill.

Centrosaurus

(sen-tro-SOR-us) had a long horn on its nose. It had very short horns over its eyes. Its frill had small spikes. Two of these spikes curled forward.

Styracosaurus

(sty-rak-oh-SAWR-us) had a long horn on its nose, but no horns above the eyes. The frill had at least four long spikes.

DID YOU KNOW?

Triceratops is the official state dinosaur of Wyoming. It is also the official fossil of South Dakota.

Triceratops had one of the largest skulls ever. It was almost one-third of its body.

In 2002 fossil collectors found a Triceratops fossil in Wyoming. This discovery showed that Triceratops's skin had bumps on it. The bumps were 1.5 to 2 inches (3.8 to 5 centimeters) across. Triceratops also had scales, like those found on a crocodile's belly.

EXTINCTION

Many scientists think an asteroid hit Earth 66 million years ago. The asteroid probably caused the dinosaurs to become extinct.

The asteroid would have thrown enough dirt into the air to block the sunlight. Plants and animals can't live without sunlight.

Scientists think the asteroid that hit Earth was 6 miles (9.7 km) wide!

The crash could also have started
deadly earthquakes and tsunamis.

Triceratops was one of the
last Mesozoic dinosaurs to
become extinct.

TYRANNOSAURUS REX

name: Tyrannosaurus rex
(also known as T. rex)

how to say it: tie-RAN-uh-SAW-rus REKS

when it lived: Cretaceous Period, Mesozoic Era

what it ate: meat

size: 40 feet (12 m) long
15 feet (4.6 m) tall
weighed 6 tons

Tyrannosaurus rex is one of the most famous dinosaurs. This "king of the tyrant lizards" is known for its enormous size and strength.

MIGHTY MONSTER

powerful, heavy tail

strong upper legs

blue whale

T. rex

Brachiosaurus

T. rex may have been mighty, but it was not the biggest dinosaur. That award goes to sauropods such as Brachiosaurus or Argentinosaurus. And while dinosaurs were the biggest land animals of all time, blue whales are even bigger. They are the largest animals ever known to live on Earth.

KING OF THE CRETACEO

Tyrannosaurus rex lived during the late Cretaceous Period, 68–66 million years ago. It was king of the northern continents. T. rex walked with other dinosaurs such as Edmontosaurus and Triceratops.

DINOSAUR ERA

TRIASSIC   JURASSIC

millions of
years ago   250   200

Other land animals in the Cretaceous Period included turtles, crocodiles, lizards, snakes, small mammals, and more birds than ever before. The sky was also busy with large and small flying reptiles called pterosaurs.

T. REX'S WORLD

During the Cretaceous Period, the continents and oceans were beginning to look more like they do today. Tyrannosaurus rex lived in what is now western North America and eastern Asia.

Earth during the Cretaceous Period

This is a T. rex fossil site in Montana.

The Cretaceous climate worldwide was very hot and wet. Sea levels were at an all-time high. Flowering plants like magnolias, ficus, and sassafras quickly grew among the evergreen forests of the Jurassic Period.

Fossils of T. rex and its close relatives have been found in Canada and the states of Montana, South Dakota, Texas, Utah, and Wyoming in the U.S.

CRETACEOUS CARNIVOR|

Tyrannosaurus rex was a fierce hunter. It likely ate any meat it could find—dinosaurs, lizards, or mammals. There is even evidence that this dinosaur may have eaten other T. rexes.

Scientists think that T. rex could grab up to 500 pounds (225 kg) with its jaws. It was so powerful that it would eat its prey, bones and all!

HUNGRY HUNTER

A few scientists think Tyrannosaurus rex was a scavenger and ate dead animals. But most agree it was a carnivore that usually hunted live prey. Fossil discoveries support this theory.

· A Triceratops fossil was found with T. rex tooth marks.

· This fossil of an Edmontosaurus tail was likely wounded by a Tyrannosaurus rex. The Edmontosaurus healed, which tells us T. rex attacked it while it was alive.

That doesn't mean T. rex would pass up free meat from a dead animal if it found one!

T. rex's forward-facing eyes helped it see and chase moving prey.

TERRIFYING TEETH

T. rex was known for its bone-crushing teeth—it had 60 of them! Adult humans have only 32 teeth. Tyrannosaurus rex lost and re-grew teeth throughout its life.

Each tooth had a job to do:

The front teeth held the prey and pulled its flesh.

The side teeth cut and ripped

The back teeth chopped and pushed food to the back of the throat.

T. rex teeth were 7.5 to 12 inches (19 to 30 cm) long. Some scientists believe T. rex had the most powerful bite of any land animal ever.

POWERFUL TAIL

Scientists once thought T. rex stood upright like a kangaroo, with its tail dragging behind. But most fossilized dinosaur tracks show no evidence of the tail dragging.

Scientists now believe T. rex stood horizontal. Its large, powerful tail on one end helped balance its huge head on the other end.

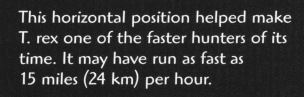

This horizontal position helped make T. rex one of the faster hunters of its time. It may have run as fast as 15 miles (24 km) per hour.

TINY ARMS

It may seem odd that a dinosaur as big as T. rex had such small arms. They couldn't even reach its mouth. But the muscles of T. rex's arms, shoulders, and chest were very strong. Scientists know this by studying the parts of the skeleton where the muscles connected.

So how did T. rex get up if it fell over? The likely answer is the same way a bird would. With the help of its tail, T. rex simply put its feet under the center of its body. Then it used its great leg muscles to stand.

T. rex had two clawed fingers on each arm.

A FOSSIL NAMED SUE

The Field Museum of Natural History in Chicago is home to the largest, most complete skeleton of a Tyrannosaurus rex ever found.

Sue's skeleton weighs 3,922 pounds (1,779 kg). Her skull alone weighs 600 pounds (272 kg)!

The fossil is named for Sue Hendrickson, the scientist who discovered it near Faith, South Dakota, in 1990. The skeleton has helped scientists understand much about this dinosaur.

Sue's skull shows us that T. rex had a very good sense of smell. The two parts of the brain responsible for smell were about the size of grapefruits.

FEATHERED FRIENDS

Tyrannosaurus rex was related to some feathered dinosaurs. In fact, paleontologists think that young T. rexes had feathers but lost them as they got older.

Adults were likely covered with scales. But they may have also had downy feathers on their backs, necks, and the tops of their heads.

T. rex wasn't the only dinosaur believed to have feathers. Archaeopteryx, from the late Jurassic Period, is often called the first bird.

SURPRISING RELATIVES

Bone fossils have allowed scientists to closely study the makeup of a T. rex. The studies led researchers to believe that the T. rex group and birds share a common ancestor.

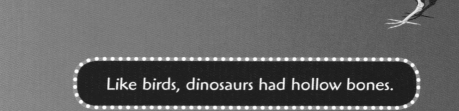

Like birds, dinosaurs had hollow bones.

Most scientists believe that all dinosaurs laid eggs. Some dinosaurs even had nests, which they likely protected the same way birds do.

GONE

Tyrannosaurus rex was one of the last Mesozoic dinosaurs on Earth.

Mesozoic dinosaurs have been gone for about 66 million years. But we are still finding new fossils and learning new things about their lives every day.

VELOCIRAPTOR

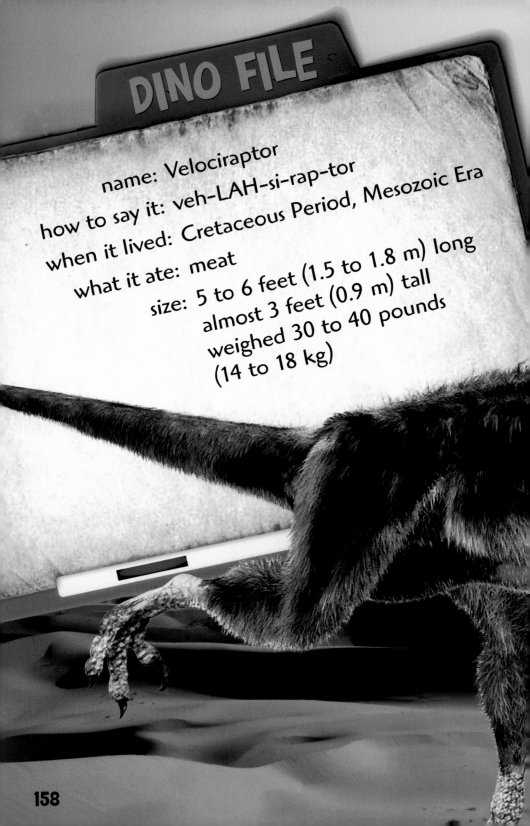

name: Velociraptor

how to say it: veh-LAH-si-rap-tor

when it lived: Cretaceous Period, Mesozoic Era

what it ate: meat

size: 5 to 6 feet (1.5 to 1.8 m) long
almost 3 feet (0.9 m) tall
weighed 30 to 40 pounds
(14 to 18 kg)

158

Velociraptor lived 75 million to 71 million years ago. The fierce meat eater was smaller than many other dinosaurs during this time.

A LARGE BIRD

long, stiff tail

Velociraptor was about as tall as a Great Dane. But it was much slimmer.

a sickle claw on each foot

flat, long head

sharp teeth

three fingers on
each hand

feathers on arms
and body

*"If animals like Velociraptor were
alive today, our first impression
would be that they were just very
unusual-looking birds."*
—paleontologist Mark Norell

THE RAPTOR GROUP

Velociraptor was part of a group of dinosaurs called raptors. The raptor group had many other dinosaurs in it.

Oviraptor (OH-vih-rap-tor) was about the same size as Velociraptor. Its skeleton was found in a nest of dinosaur eggs, so scientists named it "egg thief." Later scientists discovered the eggs belonged to Oviraptor.

Deinonychus (dye-NON-ih-kus) lived in packs and hunted small and even large dinosaurs.

Deinonychus was about the size of a mountain lion.

Achillobator (a-KILL-oh-bay-tor) was bigger than Deinonychus. It grew to almost 20 feet (6 m) long and weighed 500 to 1,000 pounds (225 to 450 kg).

Utahraptor (YOU-tah-rap-tor) is the biggest raptor discovered so far. It grew to about 23 feet (7 m) long and weighed almost 1 ton. Its sickle claw was 12 inches (30.5 cm) long.

Utahraptor was named after Utah, the state where it was found.

FEATHERS

Scientists discovered quill knobs on Velociraptor's arm in 2007. Quill knobs prove the dinosaur had feathers.

Male Velociraptors may have had brightly colored feathers. Bright feathers helped attract a mate.

Female Velociraptors likely had dull feathers. Females could have spread their feathers over their eggs. This would have hid the eggs from sunlight and predators.

Velociraptor's feathers didn't help it fly. Its arms were too short and its body was too long to get off the ground. Some birds today can't fly either, such as ostriches and penguins.

STIFF TAIL

Velociraptor's tail was stiff and stuck straight out. It helped Velociraptor keep its balance when walking or running.

When Velociraptor moved, its tail swung
back and forth. The swinging tail helped
the dinosaur change directions quickly
when it ran. Velociraptor might have been
able to do amazing twists and turns to
escape predators or catch prey.

FAST RUNNER

Velociraptor's slim body and long legs may have made it a fast runner. Speed allowed Velociraptor to catch its next meal and escape hungry predators.

Many scientists believe Velociraptor ran as fast as 24 miles (39 km) per hou Other scientists don't agree that the dinosaur was a fast runner. They think Velociraptor's long legs helped it climb and jump.

Velociraptor's name means "swift thief."

SICKLE CLAW

Velociraptor had sharp claws on its hands and feet. The second toe of each foot had an especially large claw called a sickle claw. To keep the claw sharp, Velociraptor held it up above the ground when it walked or ran.

The sickle claw could break through skin and hold onto prey. But it wasn't strong or sharp enough to kill another dinosaur.

Birds of prey, such as hawks and eagles, also have a larger claw on their second toes.

HUNTING FOOD

Velociraptor was a carnivore.
Carnivores eat meat.

This dinosaur was a good hunter. Its eyes faced
forward, which gave it great eyesight. Sneaking
up on prey was an easy task. When Velociraptor
attacked, its large sickle claw helped hold onto
prey. Its razor-sharp teeth helped kill the animal

Velociraptors may have hunted in packs. Working together would have allowed them to attack larger prey.

Because of its size, Velociraptor probably ate small dinosaurs, lizards, and insects. It may also have eaten the eggs of other dinosaurs.

It is likely Velociraptor was also a scavenger. It would wait for a big predator to finish eating its kill. Then it could rush in to eat what was left.

VELOCIRAPTOR'S HOME

Velociraptor lived during the Cretaceous Period.
It made its home in the desert areas of what is
now Mongolia, China.

Velociraptor's home was hot and dry. Water and
plants could be found in only a few places. Sand
stretched out across the land. Sometimes giant
sand dunes formed. There were also volcanoes.

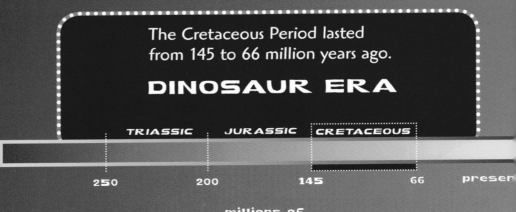

The Cretaceous Period lasted
from 145 to 66 million years ago.

DINOSAUR ERA

TRIASSIC   JURASSIC   CRETACEOUS

250   200   145   66   presen

millions of
years ago

GROWING UP

Scientists haven't found many clues about
what Velociraptor was like growing up.

Other dinosaurs in the raptor group took care of their young. That probably means Velociraptor did too.

Young Velociraptor had larger eyes and a shorter snout than adults.

Oviraptor with its eggs

DISCOVERY

Paleontologist Roy Chapman Andrews discovered the first Velociraptor fossils. He found them in the Gobi Desert of Mongolia in the 1920s. Velociraptor bones have only been found in Mongolia. But other raptors have been found all over the world, including the United States.

Andrews and his team found other dinosaurs as well, including Oviraptor. They also discovered the first dinosaur eggs.

Roy Chapman Andrews

Gobi Desert

Mongolia

FOREVER IN BATTLE

Paleontologists made an amazing fossil find in the Gobi Desert in 1971. A Velociraptor and a Protoceratops were found locked in battle. Velociraptor was holding onto the Protoceratops's head. Its sickle claw was sunk into the dinosaur's chest. Protoceratops was biting Velociraptor's right arm, which was broken. They died in the middle of the fight.

This was the first fossil discovery to show two dinosaurs fighting each other.

Protoceratops ▼

▲ Velociraptor

Some scientists think the fighting dinosaurs died when a strong wind blew a sand dune on top of them.

DID YOU KNOW?

A bone in Velociraptor's eye shows it might have been nocturnal. That means it hunted at night and slept during the day.

The 1993 movie *Jurassic Park* made Velociraptor famous. But the movie's dinosaur did not look like Velociraptor. This dinosaur didn't have feathers. It was also much bigger and smarter than Velociraptor was. The dinosaur in the movie was based on the body of a large Deinonychus.

Like birds today, Velociraptor had hollow bones. It was also probably warm-blooded.

Toronto, Canada's, professional basketball team is named the Toronto Raptors.

OTHER PREHISTORIC ANIMALS

JURASSIC PERIOD

Allosaurus

Brachiosaurus

Diplodocus

Camptosaurus

Stegosaurus

CRETACEOUS PERIOD

Tyrannosaurus rex

Ankylosaurus

Ceratosaurus

Apatosaurus

Camarasaurus

Archaeopteryx

Triceratops

Protoceratops

Oviraptor

187

GLOSSARY

armor—bones, scales, and skin that some animals have on their bodies for protection

asteroid—a large rock that travels through space

attract—to get the attention of something or someone

carnivore—an animal that eats meat

cast—an object made by pouring liquid into a mold and letting it harden

climate—average weather of a place throughout the year

conifer—a tree with cones and narrow needles

continent—one of Earth's seven large landmasses

cycad—a plant shaped like a tall pineapple, with a feathery crown of palmlike leaves

defense—an ability to protect oneself from harm

earthquake—a strong shaking or trembling of the ground

evidence—information, items, and facts that help prove something to be true or false

extinct—no longer living; a species that has died out, with no more of its kind left

fern—a plant with long, thin leaves known as fronds

ficus—a shrubby tree

fossil—evidence of life from the geologic past

frill—a large, bony plate that grows from the back of the skull

gastrolith—stomach stones used for grinding up food

geologist—a scientist who studies rocks to learn how the earth has changed over time

ginkgo—a tree with green, fan-shaped leaves

herbivore—an animal that eats only plants

herd—a group of animals that lives or moves together

hollow—empty on the inside

Jurassic Period—the second period of the Mesozoic Era; when birds first appeared

landmass—a large area of land

magnolia—a tree or large shrub that has large flowers

mate—the male or female partner of a pair of animals

Mesozoic Era—the age of dinosaurs, which includes the Triassic, Jurassic, and Cretaceous periods; when the first birds, mammals, and flowers appeared

nocturnal—active at night and resting during the day

nostrils—openings in the nose used to breathe and smell

paleontologist—a scientist who studies fossils

Pangaea—a landmass believed to have once connected all Earth's continents together

plate—a flat, bony growth

predator—an animal that hunts other animals for food

prey—an animal hunted by another animal for food

quill knob—a round bump on a bone that holds a feather

sand dune—hills of sand, made by wind and water

sassafras—a tree in North America

sauropod—a member of a group of closely related dinosaurs with long necks, thick bodies, and long tails

scavenger—an animal that feeds on animals that are already dead

shingle—a flat, thin piece of wood or other material used to cover roofs

sickle—a sharp, curved edge that is shaped like the letter C

snout—the long front part of an animal's head; it includes the nose, mouth, and jaws

supercontinent—a large continent that broke into Earth's seven continents

trackway—a set of footprints from long ago found in rocks

Triassic Period—the earliest period of the Mesozoic Era; when dinosaurs first appeared

tropical—hot, wet, and humid

tsunami—a very large wave

tyrant—a cruel ruler

Smithsonian Little Explorer is published by Capstone Press,
1710 Roe Crest Drive, North Mankato, Minnesota 56003
www.mycapstone.com

Library of Congress Cataloging-in-Publication Data
Library of Congress Cataloging-in-Publication data is available on the Library
of Congress website.
ISBN 978-1-5435-5860-9 (hardcover)

Editorial Credits
Michelle Parkin, editor; Sarah Bennett, designer; Tracy Cummins, media researcher;
Kathy McColley, production specialist

Our very special thanks to Matthew T. Miller, Museum Technician (Collections Volunteer
Manager) in the Department of Paleobiology at the National Museum of Natural History,
Smithsonian Institution, for his review. Capstone would also like to thank Kealy Gordon,
Product Development Manager, and the following at Smithsonian Enterprises: Ellen Nanney,
Licensing Manager; Brigid Ferraro, Vice President, Education and Consumer Products; and
Carol LeBlanc, Senior Vice President, Education and Consumer Products.

Image Credits
Alamy: Moviestore Collection Ltd, 65, Sergey Krasovskiy/Stocktrek Images, 122–123;
Bridgeman Images: Private Collection/© Look and Learn, 76–77; Capstone: Illustrated by
Ali Nabavizadeh, 87 Inset, James Field, 121 Bottom, 126–127, 162 Top, Jon Hughes, 1, 4–5,
6–7, 8–9, 10–11, 13, 14–15, 16–17, 18–19, 20–21, 22–23, 24–25, 38–39, 44–45, 46–47, 47 Inset,
50, 51, 52, 53, 57 Inset, 62–63, 66–67, 68–69, 72–73, 74, 82–83, 84–85, 86 Inset, 86–87, 90–91,
96–97, 98–99, 100–101, 105, 110, 111, 112–113, 115, 124–125, 156–157, 158–159, 160–161, 163 Top,
164–165, 168–169, 170–171, 175 Inset, 179 Top, 182, Back Cover, Cover, Design Element, Steve
Weston, 33 Inset, 78–79, 107, 178; Corel: 80, 81, Design Element; Creatas Images: 100 Inset;
Dr. Jack Share: 29 Inset; Dreamstime: Cata37, 160 Inset, Cmindx, 148–149, Elena Duvernay,
144–145, Peterpolak, 106, Welcomia, 94 Inset; Getty Images: Corbis/VCG, 143 Inset Bottom,
De Agostini, 11 Inset, Field Museum Library, 30, 31, Jonathan Blair, 102, Mark Hallett Paleoart,
146–147, Paul A. Souders/Corbis/VCG, 119 Inset, Richard Ellis, 130 Inset, Stocktrek Images/
Corey Ford, 58, The Print Collector, 32–33, Tim Boyle, 59; iStockphoto: leonello, 135, MR1805,
42–43, JonathanLesage, 152 Left, milehightraveler, 28–29; Karen Carr: Illustration by Karen
Carr, 132–133; Library of Congress/Prints and Photographs Division: 70 Inset, 118 Inset, 181
Inset; Luis V. Rey: 153 Top; National Geographic Creative: Michael W. Skrepnick, 150–151;
Newscom: AFP/AMNH/D.Finnin, 183, Photoshot/VW PICS/Sergi Rebordo, 61, SOLO
Syndication/Mark Large, 143, Universal Images Group/De Agostini Picture Library, 41,
Universal Studios, 185 Top, Zuma Press/Action Images/Paul Harding, 185 Bottom; Palm
Beach Museum of Natural History: Robert DePalma, 138 Bottom Left, 138 Bottom Right;
Peabody Museum of Natural History, Yale University, 28 Inset, 71 Inset; Richard A. Paselk:
23 Inset; Science Source: Francois Gohier, 12, 134, Gary Hincks, 134 Inset, Jose Antonio Penas,
174–175, Julius T. Csotonyi, 36–37, 179 Bottom, Mark Boulton, 103, Mark Hallett Paleoart,
88–89, Richard Bizley, 190–191; Shutterstock: Alexonline, 152 Right, andrea crisante, 140–141,
BACO, Design Element, Bob Orsillo, 137 Inset, Burben, 155 Right, Catmando, 25 Inset, 54–55,
56–57, 162 Bottom, 163 Bottom, chiakto, 158–159 Background, 181, Chris Fourie, 104 Inset,
Computer Earth, 116–117, corlaffra, 94–95, David Steele, 55 Inset, Designua, 76 Inset, DM7,
142, 145 Inset, ducu59us, 144–145 Background, dvektor, Design Element, eva_mask, 34–35,
Four Oaks, 9 Inset, Horse Crazy, 113 Inset, Ian 2010, 82 Inset, Juancat, 164 Inset, leonello
calvetti, 108–109, 136–137, Design Element, Linda Bucklin, 48–49, 121 Top, 172–173, Luka
Hercigonja, 53 Inset, Mahathir Mohd Yasin, 123 Inset, Michael Rosskothen, 40, 120 Bottom,
120 Top, 184, nmedia, 155 Middle, Paul Banton, 39 Inset, Photobank gallery, 128–129, pinare,
Design Element, Ralf Juergen Kraft, 151, Design Element, Robert Adrian Hillman, Design
Element, Sebastial Kaul, 124 Inset, Simon_g, 114, Sofia Santos, 130–131, Stefanina Hill,
Design Element, Steffen Foerster, 7 Inset, Design Element, Syrus Neilson, 13 Inset, T4W4,
Design Element, The_Pixel, 70–71, 118–119, 180-181 Bottom, Viktorya170377, Design Element,
withGod, 171 Bottom; StoneCompany.com: embryo model by William Monteleon, Photo
courtesy of StoneCompany.com, 27; SuperStock: Stocktrek Images, 138–139, 154–155, 166–167,
168 Inset, 177; Visuals Unlimited: Ken Lucas, 153 Bottom, Scott Berner, 19 Inset; www.
dinosauriainternational.com: 92; 93 Bottom, 93 Inset Top

INDEX